EASTER BUDS ARE SPRINGING

❀ Poems for Easter ❀

selected by Lee Bennett Hopkins
illustrations by Tomie de Paola

Harcourt Brace Jovanovich
New York and London

Also edited by Lee Bennett Hopkins
HEY-HOW FOR HALLOWEEN!
SING HEY FOR CHRISTMAS DAY!
GOOD MORNING TO YOU, VALENTINE
BEAT THE DRUM: Independence Day Has Come
MERRILY COMES OUR HARVEST IN: Poems for Thanksgiving
TO LOOK AT ANY THING

Copyright © 1979 by Lee Bennett Hopkins
Illustrations copyright © 1979 by Tomie de Paola

Every effort has been made to trace the ownership of all copyrighted material and
to secure the necessary permissions to reprint these selections. In the event of any
question arising as to the use of any material, the editor and the publisher, while
expressing regret for any inadvertent error, will be happy to make the necessary
correction in future printings. Thanks are due to the following for permission to
reprint the copyrighted materials listed below:

THOMAS Y. CROWELL for "Easter's Coming" from *Skip Around the Year* by
Aileen Fisher. Copyright © 1967 by Aileen Fisher.

CURTIS BROWN, LTD. for "Easter" by Lee Bennett Hopkins. Copyright ©
1979 by Lee Bennett Hopkins.

DOUBLEDAY & COMPANY, INC., for "Easter" by Joyce Kilmer. Copyright 1914
by Harriet Monroe from *Poems, Letters and Essays* by Joyce Kilmer.

AILEEN FISHER for "Easter Morning" from *That's Why*, Thomas Nelson & Sons,
N.Y., 1946, and copyright renewed 1974.

FRAN HARAWAY for "Back Yard: Before the Egg Hunt." Used by permission
of the author who controls all rights.

CHB

HARCOURT BRACE JOVANOVICH, INC., for "Easter Eggs" by Harry Behn from *Windy Morning*, copyright, 1953, by Harry Behn.

MARGARET HILLERT for "Easter Gift" and "At Easter Time." Used by permission of the author who controls all rights.

BOBBI KATZ for "Patience." Used by permission of the author who controls all rights.

ALFRED A. KNOPF, INC., for "My Easter Tree" from *Whisperings and Other Things* by Dahlov Ipcar. Copyright © 1957 by Dahlov Ipcar.

LITTLE, BROWN AND COMPANY for excerpts from "Easter Morning—1" and "Easter Morning—3" from "Easter Morning: *Three Poems*" by David McCord from *Away and Ago*. Copyright © 1968, 1971, 1972, 1973, 1974 by David McCord.

MACMILLAN PUBLISHING COMPANY, INC. for "Easter" by Elizabeth Coatsworth from *Twelve Months Make a Year* by Elizabeth Coatsworth. Copyright 1943 by Macmillan Publishing Co., Inc., renewed 1971 by Elizabeth Coatsworth Beston; and for selections from "An Easter Carol" by Christina G. Rossetti from *Poetical Works* by Christina G. Rossetti.

McINTOSH AND OTIS, INC., for "What If" by Myra Cohn Livington from *A Crazy Flight and Other Poems*. Copyright © 1969 by Myra Cohn Livingston.

PANTHEON BOOKS for "Easter Lily" by Mary Britton Miller. From *A Handful of Flowers* by Mary Britton Miller. Copyright © 1959 by Pantheon Books, a division of Random House, Inc.

G. P. PUTNAM'S SONS for "The Easter Rabbit" from *All Together* by Dorothy Aldis. Copyright 1925, 1926, 1927, 1928, 1934, 1939, 1952 by Dorothy Aldis; renewed.

First edition
B C D E

Library of Congress Cataloging in Publication Data
Main entry under title:

Easter buds are springing.

Includes index.
SUMMARY: A collection of 19 poems celebrating Easter.
1. Easter—Juvenile poetry. [1. Easter—Poetry] I. Hopkins, Lee Bennett. II. De Paola, Thomas Anthony.
PN6110.E2E16   821'.008'033   78-10888
ISBN 0-15-224705-X

To my Mother—Gertrude Thomas Hopkins—
who taught us to love the Holidays

ALLELUIA

The world itself keeps Easter Day,
  And Easter larks are singing;
And Easter flowers are blooming gay,
  And Easter buds are springing.
    Alleluia, alleluia.

John M. Neale

EASTER'S COMING

Through the sunshine,
through the shadow,
down the hillside,
down the meadow,
little streams
run bright and merry,
bursting with the news
they carry,
singing, shouting,
laughing, humming,
"Easter's coming,
Easter's coming!"

Aileen Fisher

EASTER

On Easter morn,
On Easter morn,
The sun comes dancing up the sky.

His light leaps up;
It shakes and swings,
Bewildering the dazzled eye.

On Easter morn
All earth is glad;
The waves rejoice in the bright sea.

Be still and listen
To your heart
And hear it beating merrily!

Elizabeth Coatsworth

EASTER MORNING

We went out on an Easter morning
Under the trees and the wide blue sky,
Up to the hill where the buds were
    swelling—
Mother, Father, and Puck and I.

And I had hopes that we'd see a rabbit,
A brown little one with a cotton tail,
So we looked in the woods and under the
    bushes,
And followed what seemed like a rabbit
    trail.

We peeked and poked. But there wasn't a
  rabbit
Wherever we'd look or wherever we'd go—
And then I remembered, and said,
  "NO WONDER,
Easter's their busiest day, you know!"

Aileen Fisher

from
EASTER MORNING—1

Question: What kind of rabbit can an Easter rabbit be?
What is the rabbit's habitat? A regular rabbitry?
We pause ten minutes now, while I consider this.
    Let's see.

In the first place, have you evidence that Easter
    rabbits *do*
Exist? You have? Who else would hide, you say, those
    eggs for you?
Who else indeed! Good point! But do they have a
    working crew?

That is: What makes you *think* those special rabbits
    are a breed?
Take Santa Claus. It seems that only one is all we need.
Why not *one* Easter rabbit, then? He's surely got
    more speed

Than Santa. And he likewise has no chimney
    problems. No,
He doesn't have a hole, of course, for he doesn't have
    to go
To the Duchess's tea party. And he has no
    Christmas flow
Of letters, asking for this and that: eggs are all you get.
The best that I can think of is, that since we've
    never met
This Easter rabbit, keep on trying. You just may meet
    him yet.

David McCord

THE EASTER RABBIT

The Easter Rabbit keeps a very
Cheerful hen that likes to lay
Blue and red and green and yellow
Eggs for him on Easter day.

He puts the eggs inside his basket
With a lot of other things—
Bunnies with pink ears and whiskers,
Little ducks with tickling wings.

Then on tiptoe he comes hopping,
Hiding secrets everywhere—
Speckled eggs behind the mirror,
Sugar bird-nests in the chair.

If we saw him we would give him
Tender lettuce leaves to eat—
But he slips out very softly
On his pussywillow feet.

Dorothy Aldis

WHAT IF

Oh, what if the Easter Bunny
    should shed his pink ears?
    his white fur?
    should leap away?
    never leaving an egg?
    never weaving a basket?
Oh, what if the Easter Bunny
    should turn into a
    March Hare?

Myra Cohn Livingston

from
AN EASTER CAROL

Spring bursts today,
For Christ is risen and all the earth's at play.

Christina G. Rossetti

AT EASTER TIME

The little flowers came through the ground,
      At Easter time, at Easter time;
They raised their heads and looked around,
      At happy Easter time.
And every pretty bud did say,
      "Good people, bless this holy day,
For Christ is risen, the angels say
      At happy Easter time."

The pure white lily raised its cup
    At Easter time, at Easter time;
The crocus to the sky looked up
    At happy Easter time.
"We'll hear the song of Heaven!" they say,
    "Its glory shines on us today.
Oh! may it shine on us alway
    At holy Easter time!"

'Twas long and long and long ago,
    That Easter time, that Easter time;
But still the pure white lilies blow
    At happy Easter time.
And still each little flower doth say,
    "Good Christians, bless this holy day,
For Christ is risen, the angels say
    At blessed Easter time!"

Laura E. Richards

AT EASTER TIME

All in the first glad days of spring
I'll set about my Eastering.
Up hill, down hollow,
Quick to follow
Where rabbits caper in a ring
Under the moon.

And soon,
After moonset and sunrise,
I'll turn my eyes
To speckled eggs and birds newborn,
Cradled by song in the early morn;
And after sudden showers
Taste flowers wet with rain.

Then,
When the bells of Easter ring,
And Easter choirs sing,
I'll take my place,
Cathedral windows rainbowed on my face.

Margaret Hillert

from
EASTER MORNING—3

Oh, Easter means
The goddess of the spring
Who supervised the gardens, greens,
Birds, flowers, everything.

But Easter, oh, it means much more:
Christ risen from the dead;
His spirit in the heart before
We lose it in the head;

The resurrection of our love,
Compassion—sharing joy
In gratitude that we are of
This world: a girl, a boy.

David McCord

EASTER LILY

If I gave you a flower
Lovely and chilly,
With petals of frost
And an ice-green well,
Would you know that I offered
An Easter lily
And begged you to drink
Its cool Easter smell?

Mary Britton Miller

EASTER

Purples,
    pinks,
        yellows,
            greens—

The prettiest hues ever seen.

Like carousel-colors
they
leap
and
play;

Easter
is
a
            day!

Lee Bennett Hopkins

BACK YARD: BEFORE THE EGG HUNT

Lilacs, dressed for Easter,
Stand silently beside
The basement stair—purpling there;
What do they have to hide?

Willow branches touch the ground—
An early morning weep;
Yellow, green and in between—
What secrets do they keep?

By the fence tall grasses grown,
Morning glories, too.
Blues and reds, nodding their heads—
What do they keep from view?

Soon, I'll search beside the fence,
The willow and the stair;
I'll look hard throughout the yard—
I'll find what's hiding there.

Fran Haraway

EASTER EGGS

Who in the world would ever have guessed
Over our garden wall toward town
Under the grass there's a cozy nest
Woven of weeds and twigs and down,
A nest with a pair of blue eggs in it
Spotted a little with brown.

It might be the nest of a wren or a linnet,
Is what my father said to me
As he smiled at the morning sun for a minute
And looked way up in a leafy tree,
A tree where he really thought it best
For the nest of a bird to be.

And he guessed if children looked and found
An Easter bunny hopping round
With a basket of colored eggs this season
That very well might be the reason
For a nest in the grass on the ground.

Harry Behn

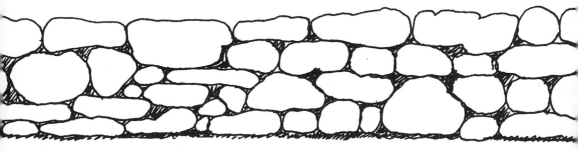

MY EASTER TREE

I have an egg tree made of dreams hanging from
        snow-white twigs.
One is a dream of springtime with lilies and
        snowdrops.
And one with lady's-slippers and fern fronds.
One has small brown bunnies hopping through
        the leaves.
One egg has butterflies flying round and round it.
There is an egg with a procession of gaily stepping
        horses,
And one with spangled roosters crowing.
And another has a hen on it with all her fluffy
        baby chicks.
One egg has white ducks on it, and one has lambs
        in a green meadow.
There is one egg with birds on it, and one with
        lilies of the valley.
And one egg has a cross saying Holy, Holy, Holy.
Every egg is a different dream, and all the dreams
        are dreams of Easter.

Dahlov Ipcar

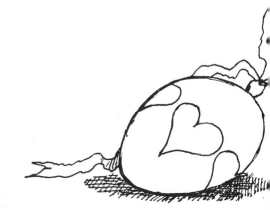

PATIENCE

Chocolate Easter bunny
    In a jelly bean nest,
I'm saving you for very last
    Because I love you best.
I'll only take a nibble
    From the tip of your ear
And one bite from the other side
    So that you won't look queer.
Yum, you're so delicious!
    I didn't mean to eat
Your chocolate tail 'till Tuesday.
    Oops! There go your feet!
I wonder how your back tastes
    With all that chocolate hair.
I never thought your tummy
    Was only filled with air!
Chocolate Easter bunny
    In a jelly bean nest,
I'm saving you for very last
    Because I love you best.

Bobbi Katz

EASTER GIFT

How would you like a rabbit,
A great big chocolate rabbit,
A rabbit full of jelly beans
All sugary and sweet?

I'd rather have a real one,
A kind of furry-feel one.
I'd give him lots of lettuce greens
And carrots for a treat.

Margaret Hillert

EASTER

The air is like a butterfly
  With frail blue wings.
The happy earth looks at the sky
  And sings.

Joyce Kilmer

INDEX OF AUTHORS AND TITLES

Aldis, Dorothy, 12
Alleluia, 5
At Easter Time (Hillert), 18
At Easter Time (Richards), 16-17

Back Yard: Before the Egg Hunt, 22-23
Behn, Harry, 24

Coatsworth, Elizabeth, 7

Easter (Coatsworth), 7
Easter (Hopkins), 21
Easter (Kilmer), 30
Easter Carol, An, 15
Easter Eggs, 24
Easter Gift, 29
Easter Lily, 20
Easter Morning, 8-9
Easter Morning—1, 10
Easter Morning—3, 19
Easter Rabbit, The, 12
Easter's Coming, 6

Fisher, Aileen, 6, 8-9

Haraway, Fran, 22-23
Hillert, Margaret, 18, 29
Hopkins, Lee Bennett, 21

Ipcar, Dahlov, 27

Katz, Bobbi, 28
Kilmer, Joyce, 30

Livingston, Myra Cohn, 13

McCord, David, 10, 19
Miller, Mary Britton, 20
My Easter Tree, 27

Neale, John M., 5

Patience, 28

Richards, Laura E., 16-17
Rossetti, Christina G., 15

What If, 13